THE MIGHTY MUSA

THE MIGHTY MUSA

JOHN TAYLOR MULDER

authorHOUSE®

AuthorHouse™
1663 Liberty Drive
Bloomington, IN 47403
www.authorhouse.com
Phone: 1-800-839-8640

Published by AuthorHouse   01/10/2013

ISBN: 978-1-4772-9510-6 (sc)
ISBN: 978-1-4772-9511-3 (e)

Library of Congress Control Number: 2012922724

DEDICATION

This book is dedicated to Judge Richard Strophy. A courageous judge who was given a choice to follow the letter of the law or the spirit of the law. A man that made a very difficult decision that best served the Olympia, Washington community.

PROLOGUE

There is one reference in the book that needs explaining:

1) Mighty Musa

In the 14th century, Kunkar Musa extended the area known as the Mellistine around Ghana to its greatest limits, making himself master of Timbukto, Gao and all of the Songhoi dominions in Africa.
Referenced by Captain L.G. Binger, Bu Niger au Golfe de Guine, & C (1852) and other authors that were considered worth citing as it relates to that time period.

I use this reference because here is an African individual that was a "king" in his country. This is not "three fifths of a person as stated in the original United States Constitution (Article 1, Section 2) which included "people of African descent". No global citizen should ever again be "categorized" as "part" of a person. But as history and current events show us, there are still individuals that consider themselves to be better than, more entitled than, of higher stature than. So in their eyes, I guess I am still "part" of a person. If someone wants to put me in "my place", I will choose for myself that place to be one of honor, integrity and respect.

For some people, honor, integrity and respect is the most important parts of their lives and they have risked everything; job, family, freedom and their lives to maintain.

If you were charged with a crime and you knew you were innocent, would you plead guilty so that you would get 30 days house arrest or would you go to trial and risk 7 years in prison.

This is a true story of an "African" American whose adversaries wanted to put him in his "place" and send him to prison. The year is 1995.

CHAPTER 1

I was one of those kids that grew up in the northwest part of the United States in a middle income family in a predominately "white" neighborhood and a "white" school system. I remember in junior high school we had a Native American girl that just blended in with the rest of us.

My dad was a school teacher and had a summer job working out at the race track where greyhound dogs chased this mechanical rabbit called "rusty" around from the start to finish line. I never did understand the greyhound-rabbit thing. One of my father's co-workers was a negro gentleman who just seemed like everyone else to me.

When I was really young I used to live out in the sunshine and my skin would turn almost black by mid-summer. I remember a neighbor commenting to me one time that I must have a lot of "pigment" in my skin. Hell, I thought she called me a "pigmy" and I went home crying to my mother. I don't think I was a racist at six years old, I just knew pygmies were really short and being "short" was not an option in my family. My dad was 6 foot 5 inches tall and was so worried I would not be taller than my mother's mom, who was only 4 foot nine inches. I think once I grew past 5 feet 6 inches my dad quit worrying about how tall I was going to be.

In high school, we had one negro football player and as far as I knew, we all got along just fine.

So to sum up my years before college, I had little or no history with "negroes" or other cultures for that matter and what I did have was never negative or an awareness of anyone being different.

When I went to college I played basketball for the University of Oregon. There were a couple of negro players on the team. On away games, I was always assigned a room with one negro player in particular. I can't say we became friends, but there was some affection between us and we loved to tease each other. I was not "insensitive" to how my fellow white players or students felt about negroes in general, and I tended to "ride the fence" when inappropriate comments were made. I wasn't mature enough nor did I have the "skills" to deal with racial issues.

One day in the locker room my "on the road roommate" was giving me a really hard time. I can't remember all that he said or did, but he finally pushed enough of my "buttons" to get me to respond.

There were probably three or four other players around at the time when I said "Lee, if you don't knock it off I am going to stick this analgesic balm up your ass and make a "fudge sickle" out of you." Looking back, my comment was very inappropriate. It was more out of affection than meanness and all of us, including Lee, laughed.

My next observations regarding "racism" came when I went into the Navy. One weekend during flight training I drove up to Jackson, Mississippi. When I stopped at a fast food restaurant I noticed negro and white kids yelling obscenities at each other. I don't ever try and look at "life" as black or white, but that was all I could see. Kids yelling at each other because they were black and white.

My next experience came when I attended advanced navy flight training in Beeville, Texas. When I first arrived at Beeville a number of the pilot group went out to get a drink. The state of Texas was a "dry" state at the time so one had to belong to a "club" to get served alcohol. We all walked into this one place and before we even sat down one of the pilots asked the manager if they served negroes at this establishment. My first thought was that this pilot was a racist. When the manager, after 'humming and hawing' around the question for a while, finally said "no we do not serve negroes here", the pilot turned around and said, "then I won't give you my business". I didn't disagree at all with what had just happened, I was just trying to understand it.

There was also a very conspicuous thing about our group of navy jet pilots. There were no negro pilots stationed with us at the time.

The navy made one lame attempt at reducing some of the racial conflict that existed on our base. I remember going to one "racial awareness" session that required mandatory attendance. I didn't have racial problems with anybody. I had to sit and listen to some negro enlisted men complain that Johnny Cash couldn't sing worth a "shit" and the white enlisted men complained about "soul music". My final thoughts on the matter were "What the f . . ."?

CHAPTER 2

After finishing my time in the navy, I eventually got hired by the Washington State Patrol. Although a predominately "white" organization, the state patrol had many cultures co-existing together into what I thought was just pretty "normal".

In 1983 I had occasion to meet the person that would become my best friend. I had just returned from Taiwan and was eager to start selling "Chinese" built sailboats as a "side job". Somebody at the State Patrol Personnel office had mentioned that there was this "black" guy in personnel that really liked sailboats and that he may be interested. As it turned out, I would meet the "brother" that I never had. I never sold any sailboats, but I would begin to understand from the outside looking in, what it was like to be a black man in America. What I didn't know at the time was the journey that was about to begin. Unfairness, injustice and racism would all raise their ugly heads in an attempt to not only destroy one man's family, but his business, his friends and his "standing" in the community that he served so well. My best friend's freedom would be on the line, and there were those in the shadows that also wanted his "soul".

It would be one black man's fight against the "white" system. One black man given the opportunity to plead guilty to a crime he didn't commit and spend a mere 30 days under house arrest, or stand his ground in the belief that he was innocent and if convicted in a court of law, spend the next 5 to 7 years in prison.

With the heart the size of a lion, with the soul of a thousand Musa warriors, and with the "cajonnes" (balls) of a complete "nut case", his journey began.

Some of his friends believed in his innocence but had distanced themselves. His family was suffering the pain and humiliation of what had happened. Everyone was waiting and watching. My friend would not be alone. It was no longer just his fight. His best friend had joined with him. Back to back, side by side, it was a battle worth fighting, no matter what the consequences.

CHAPTER 3

By 1985 I was comfortable in my job as Lieutenant and Assistant Aviation commander for the Washington State Patrol. My friend Joe had been in the state patrol personnel office for over a year and had done a "masterful" job in his consulting position. He had been praised for his insight and innovative thinking for some of the projects in the patrol that needed "desperate" changes. The desperate changes were primarily state patrol personnel records that needed to come into conformity with the rest of the state of Washington. In the past, state patrol supervisors were able to include remarks that virtually "blacklisted" employees and prejudiced an employee's ability to promote. As I recall Joe pretty much told me that all previous officer's records had just been purged and each officer virtually got a fresh start with little opportunity for any supervisor to attach personal "likes" or "dislikes".

As Joe began to "peel" the "onion skin" of state patrol politics he discovered a number of areas where the state patrol was vulnerable to potential law suits. When Joe offered comments and suggestions on this problem two things happened. The first was that upper management began to see Joe as a threat. Here was a black man who has uncovered some potential problems in the patrol. How would Joe use this information against the patrol? Secondly, for giving such sound advice with some practical solutions the patrol decided to end Joe's employment as a consultant. How could this "civilian" outsider possibly know how things worked and just bringing up potential problems would threaten all those "power" brokers trying to protect their respective empires.

It wasn't bad enough that the state patrol was letting my best friend go, there were some administrators that approached me and gave me their "sound" advice. They suggested that I distance myself from Joe in order to preserve my status and future. So I did what the state patrol asked me to do. I took their advice . . . . and promptly disregarded it.

Joe's departure was bad enough, but asking me to turn my back on my best friend just further polarized any loyalty I had with the state patrol.

I would soon be leaving the state patrol to move to California, but Joe and I would stay in touch and visit each other as often as possible.

CHAPTER 4

Joe Washington had never been in the travel business nor did he want to get in the travel business. Joe got a call from a local Olympia accountant to ask if he was interested in starting a travel agency with some financial backers in the community. Joe asked the simple question as to why does someone want me to get involved and what are they expecting in return? The answer he got was that there were some people that wanted to give something back to the community and also help minorities. That couldn't have been further from the truth. The only truth was the investors knew Joe was a positive force in the community and through that the investors had visions of carrying out their own presumptive plans.

During the height of the "affirmative" action period, it was not uncommon for whites with money and experience to find black individuals to pretend to own and run a company, while the whites controlled and ran it raking in the profits from the shadows. If the government found out about it, usually no action was taken against the white person involved.

Joe immediately rejected the idea. He knew nothing about travel agencies, had no money to invest in travel agencies, and again, had no interest in being part of a travel agency. Joe was told not to worry because the money would be provided for the travel agency and the investors would equip him with everything he needed to set up a travel office. Joe's answer was still no.

About a month later the Olympia accountant called again and once more Joe said no. Joe became angry because apparently these investors felt he was either so stupid not to know what they were up to, or worse, they didn't care if he knew what they were up to and that was to set up a "front" minority business.

Joe's anger carried for over for a week and he felt he needed to meet these people in person who were so interested in him. Joe needed for them to meet with him firsthand so there would be no misunderstanding about who Joe Washington was.

The principal investor turned out to be a successful female owner of an existing travel agency. She had fought hard against black minority business being "given" opportunities with the State of Washington without having competed or earned that right.

When the female principal investor could no longer stop this "unfair" practice of helping minorities, she decided to take another course of action. She thought she had found her black minority in Joe Washington and was going to start a "front" business in order to get her fair share of the "pie". She knew the potential profit was anywhere from one to five million dollars in gross sales per year.

After several meetings with the investor, Joe reluctantly agreed to move forward with this idea. It was also agreed that Joe would be paid a salary and he would have control of 51% of the company. Seeing huge profits on the horizon, the investor agreed to let Joe have control of the company. The first major obstacle in the process was the OMWBE, the Washington State office of Minority and Women's Business Enterprises. They immediately denied the application because they saw this for what it was, simply a "front" because Joe had not put up any of his own money. This was obviously a "dubious" enterprise. Joe was able to obtain enough of his own financing so that finally the OMWBE reluctantly issued an approval for a minority certification to do business with the state of Washington. There was one more step in the process. Joe's new company, called Essential Travel Services, had to apply to the Airline Reporting Corporation (ARC) to get permission to sell airline tickets. During the process of getting all of this figured out, Joe went to work under the tutelage of the female travel owner. The female owner, not wanting Joe to learn anything about the business, assigned him one simple task. He was to deliver the tickets to clients. Joe said "no problem" and did just that. What the female owner did not realize until later was that in addition to delivering tickets, Joe was making important contacts with this female owner's clients. Joe also began to learn everything he could about the travel business on his own. Unbeknownst to the female owner, Joe Washington had no intention of running a "front" company for anyone.

I asked Joe the following question:

Jack: Joe, knowing that you were being used, why did you continue to go ahead with establishing Essential Travel?

Joe: It had all to do with their disrespect of me or thinking that I would participate in a fraud. I only started the project to beat them at their own game, nothing more.

Joe's now very unhappy business partner, the female travel agency owner, was totally at Joe's mercy on all decision making for this new company. Forty nine percent of the company was now worthless because she had no control over the business. It would soon provide Joe with an opportunity to buy out this partner and legitimately own his own business. The female owner did not consider Joe's new business a threat to her own travel agency and both owners went on their separate ways. Joe would find other investors, but unknowingly, he would go from the "frying pan into the fire".

At about the same time Joe had been getting into the travel business, he had been asked by a friend for help in saving a fledging new community project called the Olympia Hands On Children's Museum. It had no money, no place to operate except out of donated store fronts until the owners needed them back. There was no staff, just volunteers.

This would be so typical of Joe, even though his plate was full including chairperson of the Olympia School District Vocational Advisory Board and an involvement with a proposed soccer association, Joe agreed to take on the museum project. He quickly developed a plan to stabilize the project that included reorganizing the board of directors, establish a permanent location, identify funding sources, develop the core program and hire staff. Today, this museum is one of the best in the region if not the country.

Joe's biggest financial problem since buying out his female investor was "cash flow". Since the state of Washington only paid their bills once a month, a company doing business with them would often have to wait up to 75 days to get paid. Through a local attorney, Joe found a way to borrow money each month at an unreasonable interest rate to keep his business going. Even though this was a financial strain on Joe's business, it kept the business alive for the next few years. What Joe didn't know was that his attorney was sharing Joe's business information with another client and similar to the initial investor in Joe's business, saw what the business potential was for Joe's travel agency.

When Joe was approached by this new investor and found out that he had been given information by Joe's attorney, Joe was furious. He immediately contacted an attorney in Seattle, Washington to file a lawsuit against his own attorney for unethical practices. Joe had been in business now for over five years.

There is no doubt Joe had made some enemies over the past years. He foiled an attempt by a female travel agency owner to get her share of minority state business. Joe was guilty of not letting her get away with it. He had now developed a legitimate competitive travel agency in the community. Joe, who was supposed to be the stereotype "dumb" black man in the community that didn't know "shit from shinola", was anything but. Joe's other even more deadly adversary was his own local attorney who was trying to take control of Joe's business. When Joe began the steps to take legal action against this man, the "Good old boy" system with its "puppeteers" began to pull their strings. There was no way this "uppity" black man was going to take down one of their own. Soon behind the scenes, steps were being taken to ensure Joe Washington would be "put in his place".

I asked Joe my next question:

Jack: Joe, when you were deciding to take action against your attorney, did you recognize the consequences of your actions, and if so, why did you continue with action against him, knowing that there would be serious consequences?

Joe: They knew that I knew what they were doing, and they were sure I could not do anything about it because I had no money and no one else in the area would take the case against them. My dignity was the most important thing to me, more important than my life or my freedom.

CHAPTER 5

Joe Washington was one of many people in the Olympia, Washington area that took serving the community as an honor and an obligation. On weekends you would often find Joe refereeing soccer games or putting in community service primarily helping the youth or just offering his advice to those who called on him. There were not only the youth, but businessmen, politicians and college professors just to name a few. Not everyone liked what Joe had to say, myself included, but if you listened carefully it was that cold, hard thing called "truth" that was served on a plate called "reality" and most often worth the pain of tasting it. Joe always listened and made time for everyone in need. Never patronizing, he had this ability to cut through the bullshit and get to the issues at hand. It was and still is a joy to listen to Joe's insight about anything.

Joe's travel agency, Essential Travel Service, had been doing business for over five years with some 34,000 ticket transactions per year. His office was staffed by an older, heavy set Caucasian woman who always managed the office with a smile on her face and a friendly greeting. A few of the many accounts included those for the state of Washington agencies. Somehow, two of the now over 170,000 tickets that had been issued had been mistakenly done so with credit cards from the state agencies for regular customers. On a subsequent audit, a state investigator had been sent to investigate these transactions. This is when the trouble began.

CHAPTER 6

The first time the state investigator visited Essential Travel Service, this is what the state investigator may have seen. He may have seen a black business owner employing a white female manager. During the course of several visits and with the complete help of Essential Travel, no one disagreed that the state of Washington credit card numbers had been used for non-state business. With thousands of transactions taking place, it would not be uncommon for this to happen. Essential Travel Service corrected these discrepancies by reimbursing the state of Washington for these errors. That should have been the end of it. Along with visions of promotion, many incompetent state workers would think the worst. If there were two transactions made by this company in error, there must be something "big" here to uncover. After all, the owner was black and he and his "white" manager must have something much more sinister going on. Funny thing, I had been using Essential Travel for several years without one glitch as had many others. It was always great doing business with Essential Travel and helping out my best friend.

Funny how people look at exactly the same things differently. A few errors made must be a huge conspiracy. A few errors made, two in over 170,000 transactions, not too bad.

This story isn't just about one "flawed" state investigator. It speaks of the "good old boys" that included attorneys, business adversaries and the prosecutor's office to misuse power for personal gain and to unduly influence the court.

This apparent misuse of power included a state law enforcement agency, an arrest that took away a man's presumption of innocence, an incomplete investigation, an attempt at plea bargaining that would penalize a man's right to a trial and a deluge of witnesses and documents that would so confuse and overwhelm a jury that a conviction would be forthcoming merely based on the saturation of information.

The following events are about one man's fight for survival, one man's demand for respect and one man's anger and frustration to be treated "equal" under the law. Most dramatically, it was one's man's courage and inspiration that will take his friends, associates, his own attorney and the legal system that wants to destroy him on a journey that no one is soon to forget.

It is in this story that I know hope is eternal and the only defeat any man has to suffer is in the lack of trying or simply refusing to believe in oneself. I have never been prouder to call this man my friend.

CHAPTER 7

It was late in the year and 1994 was coming to an end. The day was pretty normal, Joe's manager was doing her job in the office of Essential Travel and Joe was off at a meeting in another part of town.

About midday several Washington State Patrol cars showed up at Essential Service to arrest Joe and his office manager on four counts of theft. The State Patrol was also there to confiscate all of Essential Travel's records from the very first day of operation, over five years worth. The "probable cause" for the arrest and confiscation of records was based on a previous discovery by a state of Washington Audit that had already been corrected. The unspoken and non-existent "probable cause" was the belief that Joe had taken thousands of dollars out of his business for personal use. The arresting officer was convinced based on hearsay evidence that Joe had "cooked" the books and once the State Patrol got a chance to look at his records, his conviction would be a "slam dunk".

Since Joe was not at his office when the State Patrol arrived, his office manager asked if they would like her to call Joe to come to the office. When Joe got the call that he would be placed under arrest upon his arrival, he simply said he would be right there. For those people that were sure Joe would "run" when he found out he was about to be arrested, they couldn't have been more sorely mistaken. Joe arrived at this office a short time later and simply followed the instructions of the arresting officers.

Joe was searched as was his office manager. Having found no illegal weapons such as switch blades, guns, or weapons of mass destruction (this was a black man being arrested), Joe was asked to just wait until the officers completed their search. When all was completed, Joe and his officer manager were directed toward a female officer's patrol car. Before Joe was handcuffed he asked the female officer how the current State Patrol sexual harassment policy was working out. The female officer responded by saying that it was a very good policy and that she appreciated it. When Joe told her that he had written that policy, the female officer immediately understood what that meant. Nobody told her that she was arresting a former, fellow employee. She apologized for having to put Joe and his manager in handcuffs and made sure they were not bound too tightly. Joe and his manager spent the weekend in their respective jail cells and were released on their own recognizance the following Monday.

When I got a call from Joe a couple of days later and heard what had happened, I was furious. I immediately wrote letters to the Chief of the Washington State Patrol and to the Governor. Since all the Governor's that I had previously flown were no longer in office, I got back the usual "canned" response saying how this was normal procedure in these kind of cases . . . . yada, yada, yada. I may not have known the Governor at the time, but I did know the Chief of the Washington State Patrol. I did expect a better response from him. No one was going to convince me that my best friend, my brother, was being treated "equally" under the law. I think my thoughts were "You G . . . damn racists". It was at that moment that I knew I would do anything to help my best friend. Joe and I would later discuss many options, all of which I was willing to do. Now, however, was the time to resume our normal lives and wait. Joe's business, Essential Travel continued to operate just waiting for the "other shoe" to drop.

CHAPTER 8

In this chapter I need to take a moment and reflect on these things we call attitudes and beliefs. Look at the early settlers when the "Founding" fathers were trying to put this new country called "America" together.

People owned property. They owned land, plows, equipment and slaves. For generations this was the case. So for over a hundred years in this new country people were dealing with property issues.

In time, there was a new law in the land that created a significant change. This property called "slaves" could no longer be called property. So the question became, what status did the former slaves have now that they were declared "non-property"? If one's belief system for generations has been to look at slaves as property, how could the slaves have any status at all except to be looked at as "property not owned"? What other status could they possibly have!

Let me throw out another example that might be more meaningful for our generation. Artificial Intelligence is being developed today. Several movies have already given the populace a look at machines that all of a sudden have taken on their own independence. Most of us will struggle with this concept. How do machines fit into our legal system and will they have "equal rights", etc. I will struggle with this concept.

The point of this discussion is not to point fingers or justify the actions of our ancestors. The point of this discussion is get each of us to take responsibility for how we all look at things differently. Because of our "belief" systems, we have often "prejudiced" our ability to look at the truth. We are so intent on maintaining our belief systems that we often fail to see what goes on around us every day.

I asked Joe Washington the following questions:

Jack: Joe, why do you look at things so differently than most people?

Joe: I think because I try and see things the way they are and not the way a belief would have me see them. No matter which direction you choose, that will be the one you take action on.

Jack: Joe, from your point of view, what is wrong with belief?

Joe: My experience is that once you arrive at what you believe all other analytical thinking on the matter ends, because the word "belief" implies that you have enough information to move forward.

Jack: Joe, what is the difference between the two as you see it?

Joe: When you have seen things as they are you have "depersonalized" whatever is before you, which offers a much better quality of options from which to choose. When you just believe something, it puts you in the middle of whatever it is, so now you are dealing with two issues instead of one. You are dealing with both your own belief system and whatever the issue might be. The lines between things as they are and what we believe has always been blurred, I think more today than ever before. This is because the two lines both affect you in the same way. So if you believe "your group" is better than another group, no matter what the reason, or lack thereof, then that group can never rise above your beliefs about them. So belief, by itself, in my view is just not the best for me to take to obtain the high degree of "adjustment" that I require.

Jack: Joe, will things ever change between us?

Joe: Yes, they will get even better.

It is certainly not my intent to "attack" anyone's belief system. It is my intent to get people to consider what goes on around them from a broader point of view.

The story continues . . . .

CHAPTER 9

Joe Washington, a black man, had his entire life to review what happened to minorities in business in American society. He knew there was a history of black business owners who initially didn't keep really accurate books. So when the "power brokers" of society went after these business owners, they would know that these businesses would often have poor accounting systems in place which made them vulnerable. Joe Washington also knew that when he out-maneuvered his business partner to be sole owner of the travel business and when he began to take legal action against his own attorney, that "his" day of reckoning would be coming. What few people understood was that Joe's business plan and his life plan were the same and he already had that equation "plugged" in.

From the time Joe was a young man, he understood that to have his dignity as a man in a predominately "white" society, there would be consequences. That would become so normal to Joe and "black" society as a whole that consequences were hardly worth mentioning. Hey, if you joined the military you would expect to be in combat zones, get shot or even killed. If you are a black man, there are consequences. That fact became a mere "footnote" to those individuals who knew the importance of dignity and respect and were in extreme cases, willing to give their lives to preserve it.

So here is a quick summary of Joe Washington's business plan, or as I saw it, his "survival" plan.

Joe knew that his business, Essential Travel had to have detailed accounting and documentation for every cash or check transaction via a receipt. Each bank slip contained the amount of each transaction plus the transaction number that added up to the total amount to be deposited. In essence, every dime could be and was accounted for from the first day of business.

Joe already had a lifetime of preparation for any consequences that would occur as time went on.
Here comes the arrest.

Because Joe had prepared himself for the day of reckoning or retaliation to come, he was totally prepared for it.

Joe's preparedness was not about escape plans or duplicate books. From the moment of the phone call from Joe's office manager that an arrest was imminent, Joe's "coolness" had already begun to counter Joe's adversaries' plans. When Joe showed up at his office for his arrest, it was just another day.

Joe did now cower, he did not beg, he did not cry out "Oh please master" or any such crap as that. The adversaries in the shadows had already lost the game they were trying to play, they just didn't know it yet.

Prior to Joe's arrest, I believe the Washington State Patrol had been given false information. They were told they had to "swoop" in with a mass of patrol cars and personnel to arrest a black man that was armed and dangerous. The Patrol wasn't even told that this was a previous employee that still had friends in the patrol and also had left the patrol in good standing.

The State Patrol had been given false information in another area as well. They were led to believe that once they had Essential Travel's accounting books, it would be a "slam dunk" conviction. They couldn't have been more wrong.

As if the call was heard from the "Mighty Musa" of ancient Africa to unite his people and become "one" with Joe Washington, the path ahead was clear. Joe would stand proudly before his community and friends and accept his fate. What he would never give up was his dignity or his demand for respect.

CHAPTER 10

Before continuing with the story I will share my thoughts as I saw them from my point of view. My point of view comes from having been employed with the Washington State Patrol for 12 years, 6 as a Trooper working the highways, and 6 as a pilot and Assistant Aviation Commander flying three different Governor's, state officials and other state employees.

1) There was not enough evidence for probable cause to either make an arrest or to confiscate the accounting records from Essential Travel.

2) The probable cause could have been ascertained through a grand jury investigation, but was not.

3) I felt it was pre-mature for law enforcement just to walk in to a business unannounced and take all of Joe's business records in an attempt to find something illegal?

4) As a former Washington State Patrol Lieutenant, I can tell you that "fishing" in the state of Washington is

illegal unless you have a license. The license in this instance was called "probable cause", and in this situation, blinders must have been in place because "probable cause" did not exist.

When Joe was arrested there was an initial bail set for his release as would be expected for a serious felon. The following Monday Joe and his office manager went before a judge and ended up being released on their own recognizance. The "Shock and Awe" plan that Joe's adversaries had launched turned into a diluted conversation about "now tell me again why you are before me", said a confused judge. On the day of arraignment I had my own confusion about my ongoing struggles of why some lawyers do the things that they do. I didn't understand at the arraignment when four charges of theft in either the first or second degree were presented to the judge, why Joe's defense attorney did not bring up how the "evidence" in this case or lack thereof was obtained? That alone could have been grounds for dismissal.

The only answer that I could come up with was that there had to be a certain level of trust between the judges and the prosecutor's office. The judge had to respect the arresting document at face value and therefore set a trial date. What the prosecutor's office did not know at the time, from my point of view, was that they had also been given false information. There is a legal term called "fruits of the poisonous tree" that basically states that any evidence obtained "illegally" cannot be used in a court of law. Because of the "behind the scenes" political pressure of Joe's adversaries, no one understood that the State Patrol, the Prosecutor or the judge had all been "fooled" into thinking that there was "real" evidence that would overwhelmingly convince a jury that Joe Washington was guilty. What a grand jury would have found out was that Joe Washington had an incredibly good accounting system and that every penny was attached to a receipt or invoice. The irony of this story as it continues to unfold is that by the end of the trial, even the judge understood the lack of evidence against Joe Washington. And the judge would come to understand a lot more, and he would not be happy about it!

CHAPTER 11

The Washington State Patrol had ample staffing to go through all of the records obtained from Essential Travel. It had been assumed by all of Joe's adversaries that within 30 days enough evidence would surface to set a trial date. Well, 30 days went by, 60 days went by, and then finally 6 months had gone by. It was obvious to Joe that no evidence had been found. The State Patrol kept digging. They contacted the Internal Revenue Service, they contacted vendors with which Essential Travel did business, and they contacted a number of clients. After 6 months, this is what they found:

1) Essential Travel had used State of Washington American Express cards inadvertently for other customer business. This had already been resolved and monies were paid back to the state of Washington. (Refer chapter 6)

2) There was an Essential Travel customer that had not received a trip due to confusion on rescheduling issues.
3) Essential Travel was not up to date on repaying a couple of their vendors.

That was it. None of these charges showed the following criminal charges: . . . did wrongfully obtain or exert unauthorized control over property of another in a value in excess of $1,500, and /or by color or aid of deception, did obtain control over the property of another in a value in excess of $1,500 . . . .

That was the evidence that the state patrol came up with after 6 months of investigation. The case should have been dropped at this time.

There was such an expectation about the outcome of evidence that the state patrol and prosecutor's office must have been shocked at finding absolutely "nothing".

For whatever reason, the prosecutor's office played a "card" that should haunt them forever. Knowing there was no evidence, the prosecutor's office went before a judge, with Joe and his attorney present. They told the judge that if Joe would plead guilty to the four charges, he would only get 30 days of house arrest and that was it. If he went to trial and was found guilty, he could spend 5 to 7 years in prison. Without hesitation, Joe's response was "then I will see you in court". I don't want to even dwell on the "unfairness" of this proposal. Only a guilty person or a person without dignity would consider the lesser offer. The prosecutor's office never believed that Joe wouldn't roll over. A black man with integrity and dignity, what was that all about?

So now there would be the expense of a trial for both the taxpayers and Joe. The prosecutor's office had gambled and lost. Now they had to come up with evidence to prove their case. Joe already knew what the evidence was. He also knew that the battle had just begun to keep his dignity intact. The trial for both sides began.

CHAPTER 12

The first day of the trial was to select a jury. There would be 12 jurors and an alternate juror selected in the mix. The jury would consist of a lot of retired older folks with a few middle aged ones. There would be no blacks selected as none had come up for consideration in the random selection process.

Once the jury was selected, the prosecution made an interesting move. This was the first day of the trial and they wanted to send a message to Joe and his attorney. The message was, fine, you want to go to trial, we will add another 3 counts of theft to the already current 4 counts of theft. The counts were the same wording and the same charges as had already been resolved with the state of Washington. It was obvious to Joe and I that the prosecutor's approach was going to be through the use of "smoke and mirrors". The prosecutor's plan was simple. Give the jury more information than they can handle and confuse them with a bunch of technical jargon.

Even though Joe had a very competent attorney from Seattle, it was all I could do to not want to stretch Joe's attorney's throat out a little. The fact that this trial had even begun was a travesty.

CHAPTER 13

As a spectator in the courtroom I learned on the first day there is a certain protocol. I was advised by Joe's attorney that I had to sit on the "defense" side of the courtroom. What was this, a f . . . . wedding? So I had a nice spot picked out toward the back of the courtroom where I could observe as much as possible.

At midday, there was a break for lunch and we had about an hour and a half to eat and go over the events as they were unfolding. Joe's wife had taken a seat behind the defense table and was taking notes of the proceedings. Her primary function was to see if the prosecution had any meaningful evidence against Joe. I never sat next to Joe's wife because this lady was a serious note taker, and even though I loved her dearly, a man does not distract an educated, intelligent woman from taking notes.

The first day and a half of the proceeding went pretty much as expected. A whole lot of meaningless information that was boring me and I'm sure the jury as well. The first incident came when Joe and I were returning to the courtroom. Joe and I had been through the security station over 5 times now with just a casual inspection. Not this time. The security guard singled out Joe and wanted to give him the "wand". You know the same wand at the airport that makes you feel like the worst scum of the earth. There were 10 Caucasian people going through security with our group and Joe, oh, let me see, the black man, gets singled out. Joe's attorney was oblivious to what was going on. Joe was upset and so was I. We would get even with Joe's attorney later, if I didn't strangle him first.

We finished up the rest of the day, then met in a local attorney's office that evening. Joe got very upset with his attorney about the incident with the wand and walked outside. That is the only time in 12 years that I have seen Joe visibly angry. Joe's attorney was trying to minimize the issue by saying that what happened was not important. It couldn't have been more important. Joe was in a trial for his life because he was black and he was "wanded" because he was black. What part of this abomination didn't people understand?

Not a good first two days for Joe Washington. I am not seeing this "justice" thing going very well, but I also did not see any incriminating evidence on the first two days.

My mind set was this. I will stand by my best friend, no matter what. Show me the evidence! "You racist m . . . f . . . s, show me the evidence." I would make that statement for the remainder of the trial.

CHAPTER 14

Day 3 turned out to have an interesting twist for me. After I settled in to my spot in the back of the courtroom I had one of my former State Patrol Troopers sit next to me. He was eager to ask me a lot of questions and by the time the trooper left there would be no doubt in the Trooper's mind that I was there to support my best friend, Joe Washington.

Now remember, the state patrol was the arresting agency and state patrol officers would be getting on the stand to testify about all of the records they had obtained from Essential Travel. So now they had a former state patrol employee in the courtroom supporting a person they were "hell bent" on finding guilty. I just wasn't any former employee in their eyes.

I had been a member of the state patrol for 12 years. I was a lieutenant and assistant aviation commander of the aviation division. I had personally flown three different governors and other state officials. I was the first recipient after 88 previous nominations of the state patrol's highest award, the Award of

Honor. Did I know a lot about the state patrol? Of course I did, and then some.

This day was pretty much the same as the first two. The prosecutor called witnesses to testify and they were cross-examined. My primary focus was to pay attention to any incriminating testimony. Why a vendor got to testify was beyond me. Money owed to a vendor was not a crime the last time I checked.

Each day the prosecutor had brought in boxes and boxes of evidence. There would be a "grease" board set up with documents attached and each witness would testify to the documents. Joe's attorney was often quick to point out discrepancies in the documents. I was convinced early on in the trial that the jury would be swayed by the prosecutor's abundance of evidence, not the quality of it. Display after display, document after document was discussed. I was a trained police officer that had done enough investigations to know real evidence when I heard it. There was never any incriminating evidence that "spoke" to me during the trial. Smoke and mirrors, smoke and mirrors. If I couldn't make sense of it, how could the jury make sense of it.

Another day ended with another evening session with Joe and his attorney strategizing for the next day.

CHAPTER 15

Day 4 was much the same as day 3. This time I had a Sergeant from the State Patrol that I knew sit next to me. As pissed as I was about what was going on with the trial, I was slightly amused with the attention that I was getting from the state patrol. My first sense about the patrol was that they feared that I would be called as a witness to testify for the defense. I certainly didn't have any stuff to testify about in regards to the arresting officers and although I knew the primary investigating officer, I couldn't imagine what I would have said about him. I think it was more about the patrol being paranoid about any former employee testifying on behalf of a suspect in a felony case. Come to think of it, Joe Washington was a former employee of the state patrol. Isn't it interesting in all the data that was collected in 6 months that there was no record of Joe Washington ever working for the state patrol? Was that selective evidence collecting or what?

CHAPTER 16

Day 5 offered testimony that was of particular interest to me. The primary state patrol investigating officer was on the stand giving testimony. When the officer was asked by the prosecutor to testify as to which Essential Travel clients had been owed money, I paid attention to what he said. The officer testifying knew that I was in the courtroom when he had to read my name as a client that was owed money by Essential Travel. I couldn't believe it. There it was, a bold face lie. The state patrol never contacted me or asked me during the investigation about any money that Essential Travel apparently owed me. All they had was a client list from which they had taken names. I was so excited I passed a note to Joe to have his attorney call a recess before cross-examining the officer. I pleaded with the attorney to put me on the stand but he refused. Joe's attorney said he would use the information during the cross examination.

After court resumed, Joe's attorney asked the question specifically about my name being on the list. The officer looked at me and then said to Joe's attorney, "I may have made a mistake with that name". "I may have made a mistake with that name". That was the whole case in a nutshell. "I may have made a mistake with that name". Every piece of f . . . . "quote" evidence was a mistake. I felt Joe's attorney had an incredible opportunity to totally discredit this officer's testimony at this point in time. The jury, as well totally missed the significance of that one statement.

When I asked Joe's attorney why he didn't press that point further, his response was that he felt he would be taking on the state patrol and that would not set well with the jury. My thoughts were "what about your client, asshole"?

I always respected Joe's wishes when it came to his attorney's decisions. It wasn't my ass on trial and I certainly did not want to be the one to try and influence "bad" decisions when it came to "legaleze". But, damn, it was hard sitting there day after day listening to item after item of extraneous "bullshit" lacking any resemblance of "real" evidence.

I asked more questions of Joe:

Jack: Joe, why did you pick this very expensive attorney to defend you? It was always his way or no way.

Joe: If it seemed to you that my attorney had no real interest in me or my innocence, you would be right. I didn't need someone who believed in me, or my innocence, after all I had never left my fate in the hands of anyone but myself before. I selected him because he had one of the biggest ego's I had ever seen. It was all about him and keeping his "win-loss" intact. So my trial was more about the system versus him. As you may recall my attorney and the prosecutor put on quite a show. The outcome of the trial was never in doubt in my mind. However, he did catch the judge's eye with the quality of his lawyer skills that he exhibited, that was all I required. Because in the end my fate was always in the judge's hands.

CHAPTER 17

On day 6, I had a Lieutenant from the State Patrol sit next to me at Joe's trial. I got asked the same questions and the officers were always pleasant. These were people I had worked and partied with. It must have been difficult for them to have to come to me each day knowing that they had to ask these "bullshit" questions.

I knew in my heart by the end of the 6th day that nobody cared about Joe Washington's innocence. Nobody cared that the evidence was without substance, nobody cared that the people testifying had nothing of value to say. What I began to painfully see was a "black" man in the courtroom. I saw what the state patrol saw, what the prosecutor saw, and what the jury saw. This was not about being color blind, this was about being "colored". A "colored" black man in a courtroom being bombarded by hundreds of documents and over a hundred exhibits. Smoke and mirrors. The prosecution was proving their case by overwhelming the jury with documents and witnesses. I think Joe knew the outcome as well. He told me that he thought his own attorney believed he was guilty. So much for the presumption of innocence. Not in "Black America"

I was becoming bitter and disappointed. I felt sadness for my best friend having to go through this ordeal of "trumped" up charges in a community that he had served so well.

One of the ironies of the trial was that Joe and the presiding judge were members of the same rotary club. So on every Monday during the trial the judge and Joe would see each other in the courtroom and in rotary.

CHAPTER 18

The next few days of the trial were pretty much the same. By the last day I had a Major in the State Patrol sitting next to me. Joe was so cool that every morning he would look up my way and see who was next to me and smile. Then in the evenings Joe would say, "Damn, Jack, you had some pretty tall cotton sitting next to you today." At least we hadn't completely lost our sense of humor.

On the last day of the trial, we were all exhausted from days in the courtroom and evenings of strategizing with the attorney. In retrospect, I don't think it was as much strategizing as it was Joe's attorney telling us how "bad" Joe's case was going. Hell, we didn't need to strategize to know that.

On the following day, Joe and his office manager had been at work when they were notified that the verdict from the jury was forthcoming. Joe and his office manager appeared without Joe's attorney and listened to the verdict of guilty being given. The next phase was to be sentencing and Joe and his office manager had a few weeks to prepare for the inevitable, 5 to 7 years in prison. Joe simply went back to work and finished out his day.

If you think this is the end of the story, you are wrong. What happens next is the joining of forces of the Mighty Musa and Captain Jack. Nobody will believe what happens next. The story continues . . . .

CHAPTER 19

The following day after the verdict of guilty, Joe, his wife and myself drove to Seattle to meet with Joe's attorney. I remember sitting at this conference table on the twelfth floor of this high rise building overlooking Elliot Bay. What a spectacular view. I suppose I could have taken a picture and sent it to Joe when he went to prison just to remind him of what people treated "equal under the law" were enjoying. If the reader is wondering if I was disappointed and "pissed" about the conduct and outcome of the trial, that would be an understatement. I had to put my anger aside and focus on what was next; trying to keep Joe and his office manager from going to prison.

Joe's attorney made a statement that I will paraphrase: Joe, you were found guilty and you are going to prison. The judge is bound by certain protocol and cannot change that.

I would do everything in my power to get Joe's attorney to eat those arrogant words. He was basically telling Joe to just give up and accept his fate. Fuck that shit!

Joe and I then made the suggestion to his attorney about having prominent members of the Olympia community send letters to the judge. The attorney looked at us like we hadn't heard what he had just previously said. He totally dismissed the idea as being ludicrous. After all, he was a high priced attorney and he was convinced Joe would be going to prison no matter what thoughts we had on the matter. While the attorney was "basking" in his own arrogance, Joe and I looked at each other. It was that look of alright you arrogant son of a bitch, alright you "adversarial" assholes, alright world, the Mighty Musa and Captain Jack had a plan, we just didn't know what it was yet.

CHAPTER 20

I had been a guest in Joe and his wife's home during the trial and would remain there until the final outcome. There was not a moment went by that excluded the "pain" all of us felt during this experience. The task ahead would seem to some as unbearable and unattainable. To know that my best friend and "brother" was going to prison was "ripping" the heart out of me every day. The following days would be some of the most challenging days of my life. For us to accept the attorney's belief that Joe's situation was hopeless was "f . . . ." ludicrous. It was time to come up with the "plan".

Strategizing was never easy but we developed the following elements for our plan.

1) Put together a plan that was simple but effective.
2) Carry out the elements of the plan.
3) Stick to the plan, no matter what.

Sticking to the plan, no matter what, was to be our greatest challenge. This was not a business plan, it was to become a "Statement" plan. A statement of one man's dignity, courage and inspiration to show all of us the power of working together.

More questions for Joe:

Jack: Joe, what is your biggest regret and disappointment about America?

Joe: That I am and many others like me, are a missed opportunity to be an even greater asset to our country, and not just in a time of crisis.

Jack: Joe, where do you see America 100 years from now?

Joe: I see America continuing to reinvent itself to stay a leader among leaders, and at the same time finding new ways to make trivial things even more important, and important things still left unattended. I fear 100 years from now America will still not have discovered the nation it could become.

CHAPTER 21

The first task of the plan was to write letters to Joe's friends, customers and business associates. We wanted the letters to convey a request from each person to write a letter to the judge at Joe's trial simply stating Joe's impact on their lives and to ask the judge for leniency in regards to the impending prison sentence. We sent out a couple of hundred requests for letters. My letter would be one of them. We also asked that these same people show up on the day of sentencing to show their support for Joe.

The second task was for Joe and I to go out into the community and meet with as many people as possible prior to the sentencing date. Our impetus was this; The state patrol had been the arresting agency in Joe's case. I was a former state patrol lieutenant, their highest decorated officer and I had left the State Patrol in good standing. More importantly, I had been at the trial and could honestly say that there was no evidence presented at the trial to convict Joe and his office manager. Now, if I was representing the "fashion" police, I could certainly understand that Joe in his sport coat and cowboy boots and his office manager in her "plain" dresses would constitute several violations. I am sure that I could have come up with seven of those as well. Joe and his office manager would certainly not be making the cover of any fashion magazines.

Joe and I would leave his house early in the morning and began contacting Joe's friends and associates. This was not the "Black" community we are talking about here. This was the Olympia, Washington community of which a few black individuals were included.

We would go to places of business, we would go to individual homes and we would meet people in coffee shops. From early morning until into the evening Joe would introduce me to those people I hadn't met, or I would get reacquainted with those that I did. I would talk about my background and the events of the trial as I saw them.

I was amazed at the number of stories these people had about Joe. Joe helped one of their children stay away from drugs. Joe was a positive influence on a soccer player's life that he had coached. Joe had helped another friend go through a difficult divorce. Joe steered a young man away from thoughts of suicide and got him to consider some other positive options. Joe's help with the Children's Museum for the kids. We talked to department heads of various state agencies and they would convey how Joe had been a positive influence in their lives. Business owners would all convey the positive influence Joe had with them in the past. At one point I asked Joe if we were trying to keep him out of prison or get him nominated for "sainthood". I hope I am painting a "picture" here for the reader. No, Joe is not a saint. Isn't it interesting in the six months it took the state patrol to investigate Essential Travel's accounting records that not one day was spent into finding out who "Joe Washington the man" was? Remember, the state patrol did not or would not acknowledge that Joe was even a former employee of that agency.

So day after day, Joe and I would be meeting with people in the community. By the eighth or ninth day, we were exhausted. There was not any meeting we had that even one individual doubted Joe's innocence. There were no "what about this? statements or "looks" of disbelief in our encounters.

Our plan was simple, but Joe felt we were not doing enough. Joe wanted to pursue some other options. We had no "barometer" to see how effective our efforts had been so far. My feeling was that we had a solid plan and we needed to stick to it. Joe felt that there may be some other things we could do but when we explored them, I still felt it was necessary to stick to what we had. Remember, I am not the one going to prison. I don't know if I could ever put into words what it means to totally trust someone or to be willing to give your life for them. This was and still is the bond that Joe and I have. Knowing that my insistence about sticking to the plan may result in his going to prison, Joe agreed to continue with the current plan. For three weeks we never deviated from that plan. The routine stayed the same and we would soon find out the results of our efforts. Neither Joe or I had any expectations about the day of sentencing. We were exhausted and I was heartbroken.

CHAPTER 22

On the morning of sentencing, Joe had been told by one of his friends that worked in the prison system to leave all of his valuables at home and to wear white socks and white underwear. I would drive Joe to court that day only to watch my best friend be taken away in chains to begin his five to seven year prison sentence. My thoughts drifted to making visits to see Joe in prison and I was having problems holding back my tears.

Joe, his wife and I got out of my car for that last walk to the courtroom. Upon arriving, the courtroom was empty. There was Joe, his office manager, and Joe's attorney at the defense table. Joe's wife sat behind Joe but today no notepad. I took my seat in back, and today there would be no state patrol officer sitting next to me.

The courtroom was large enough to hold about 150 people. About five minutes before the sentencing began, the courtroom was filling up. My first thought was who are these people? Are they here for the next case, are they news media or just all of Joe's adversaries here to see the final "kill"?

Then I began to recognize the people entering the courtroom. It was the people that Joe and I had contacted over the last few weeks. Very quickly, the courtroom was overflowing. It was now standing room only.

When it came time for the judge to enter, I watched the judge's reaction to the crowd as he took his seat. I could tell the judge was not expecting this kind of crowd and he appeared to be a little nervous about that. I also noticed that the judge had brought a huge stack of documents with him. What I didn't know yet was the judge was carrying all of the letters that had been sent on Joe's behalf.

It was extremely noisy until the judge "rapped" court into session with his gavel. Then you could have heard a pin drop. The judge read a summary of the trial and also what he was "bound" to do by law. He was "bound" to send Joe and his office manager to prison.

Despite the decision by the jury, I believe the judge understood the lack of "real" evidence presented at the trial. So ask the question, if the judge understood the lack of evidence, why did he not dismiss the case regardless of the jury's verdict? The answer is not that difficult. When you operate in the "Good old boy" system, those kind of decisions can be "career breakers". One would not only "piss" off the jurors who vote, the prosecutor's office, and also the "puppeteers" that certainly can influence one's future. Now the real time question was asked, what does a judge do with a courtroom full of prominent business people and prominent citizens here to see justice served "for" Joe Washington? Not a pleasant situation for any judge.

There were to be three people allowed to speak for Joe at the sentencing. Joe, Joe's wife and myself. Joe was first to speak. Joe's words were calm, clear and concise. "Your honor, thank you for your time today. The only things I have to say are that I feel I have been treated 'unequal' under the law and that I will appeal the outcome of this trial."

There it was. The judge was about to send Joe to prison and Joe made his statement. He had the courage to stand before the judge knowing full well he would get no leniency. His dignity preserved, Joe, the Mighty Musa, was making it clear that in order to preserve that dignity, in order for him to stand up for the Black America in which he lived, he was going to say what needed to be said. He not only had previously turned down an opportunity to plead guilty with a 30 day house arrest, he was now accepting his fate as a black man in a white America.

The judge was furious and the courtroom was stunned. Isn't this the part where the defendant is supposed to show remorse? I looked around at the faces in the courtroom. The prosecutor was bemused. The faces in the courtroom showed about every emotion possible. Blank faces, open mouths, handkerchiefs wiping away tears. A multitude of faces all staring at Joe Washington and the judge. The judge did not hesitate to advise Joe that he had been given a "fair" trial (he did not use the words equal) and that he was not going to be intimidated by all the letters and people present in the courtroom.

With the judge's subsequent fury, which took about 45 minutes, my stomach was turning into knots and I was having trouble keeping back the tears.

When the judge finally finished "ranting" it was Joe's wife's turn to speak. With the advice of Joe's attorney, again, Joe's wife got up and read a prepared statement to the judge. Fuck, she may have just as well read a passage from "Dick and Jane" because it was so unmoving and dispassionate. In all fairness to her though, Joe's wife had been through too much, and there was nothing left for her to give.

Then it was my turn to get up before the judge. For the last hour my thoughts had been on Joe going to prison. How would we stay in touch, what would happen to our friendship, what would happen to Joe. With tears streaming from my eyes, I stood before the judge and I talked about Joe and what he meant to the community; an asset and a friend to all. I then asked the judge for leniency. I thanked the judge and took my seat at the back of the courtroom.

What I believe the judge was really furious about, what really became clear by the end of the trial, was that he had been used. The state patrol and the prosecutor's office had been used. It was then that the judge made a "career" influencing decision. As if time had stood still in anticipation of the judge's decision, the courtroom became "eerie", the silence taking everyone's breath away. I felt like my heart was going to explode. "The Mighty Musa did not get people to write those kind of letters if he was a man without dignity. The Mighty Musa did not get a courtroom filled with supporters if he was not a man of courage. The Mighty Musa did not get his best friend to stand with him and take on his former employer, the Washington State Patrol, without being innocent.

The next words out the judge's mouth electrified everyone in the courtroom. A summary of that statement is as follows:

It is the decision of this court that all prison time be suspended. (Now I can't control my tears.) Furthermore, both defendants will serve 500 hours of community service. (That is about 1/3 of the hours Joe serves anyway, so that works). The third stipulation was that Essential Travel would pay back any monies owed to clients mentioned in the trial. (Except me of course, because I had already pointed out that no "f . . . ." money was owed to me).

With that said, the gavel's motion ended the day of sentencing and court was over. The courtroom crowd was thrilled. The prosecutor had tried to object several times during the sentencing but to no avail. Joe's adversaries just saw their entire plan backfire in an attempt to discredit and get rid of Joe Washington. I think there was a fear by Joe's adversaries that Joe would retaliate someday. Funny thing about fear, isn't it. It is so misused and misunderstood that it either cripples or incapacitates people.

Joe's attorney was jubilant. He immediately walked over to Joe congratulating him and said, "we did it, we won." I am now officially informing that "said" attorney that you gave up on Joe. Joe's attorney did not keep Joe Washington out of jail. The Mighty Musa and Captain Jack kept Joe Washington out of jail. The Mighty Musa and Captain Jack have never looked back, except to write this story.

More questions:

Jack: Joe, how do you go about adjusting to the many complex issues and other things you face on a continuing basis?

Joe: To adjust to the important things that occur in real time, to the extent I am able, I am always aware of the "present" moment by moment, day by day.

Jack: Joe, what about the past and the future, how do they fit in your adjustment system?

Joe: They fit as what they are, resources, the past is information, nothing more. How I use that information is key, the future is an assumption, period. The present is the only time that matters to me, because it's my life in "real time. The present is the only constant I know, and the only place that I can directly effect, but the present is not the only time that can affect me. Adjusting at this stage of my life is all but automatic and it requires little or no effort on my part. Mastering the art of adjusting became my personal freedom for me and from others. In my view, life is meant to be good, but it is up to each of us to find a way that will lead us in that direction. Adjusting is my way.

During this 12 years of friendship with Joe Washington, I have had but a "glimpse" into what "Black" America could possibly be like. Joe would lose his court appeal to the higher courts, but he would have his dignity, his freedom and our friendship.

I asked Joe the following questions to continue to better understand what goes on in the two America's:

Jack: Joe, where do you see yourself in terms of black America with the African American community?

Joe: The answer to this question is easier than it might appear. If the African American community was a painting, I would fit very comfortably anywhere on the canvas you placed me, because I am completely comfortable with who I am. Couple that with my ability to adjust, permits me to move with ease across all levels of my community, without interrupting anyone's comfort zone, unless I choose to. That includes both communities, blacks and whites.

Jack: Joe, would you consider yourself mainstream in terms of your everyday life? If not, what adjustments do you feel you have to make that other blacks don't?

Joe: No, in order for me to be mainstream, I would have to be a member of the prevailing group and accepted as an equal. This group sets the mainstream agenda for the entire nation. I am not a member of that group, so I adjust to the agenda they set. My adjustments are made only in conjunction with what I wish to accomplish at any given time. The mission's I undertake are always crystal clear to me, so my efforts for each one is always at the highest level, then I stay the course all the way to the conclusion. Since adjustment is a very individual process, I can't speak for blacks as a group.

Jack: Joe, do you ever see yourself being treated the same as the non-black population in your lifetime?

Joe: There is only one truth for me in my own country, that is I will always be seen and treated differently. What my relationship with you taught me is that it does not have to be that way. When I went to China I saw for the first time in my life what it was like to be treated in the "first person". I felt an anger I had never experienced before about my country, when I realized the "intent" in its treatment of me. As you know, I was willing to lose even my family as well as my livelihood. For me nothing comes before self-respect . . . nothing. After all I am an African American, no matter where I am.

My final thoughts on this book are as follows: Having now gone beyond a sometimes "painful" glimpse into "Black America", I am angry about what I have not been told by "White America" in the history books. This enlightening experience has enabled me to see a glimmer of "racism" and "discrimination" from a black man's point of view. Where were the stories of Harlem, a New York community that told of successful black businessmen? Why did I not learn about the Tuskegee Airmen until later in my life? The stories are numerous but blatantly missing from everyday life.

Since I had been "metaphorically" color blind most of my life I have had to learn some hard life lessons about Black and White America. I understand that I don't have to sit on the sidelines and condone "unequal" justice under the law. Although I have always considered myself an advocate for my fellow employees, I choose now to be an advocate for my fellow human beings.

I understand the difference between adjusting to life or being assimilated by it. I have had my own struggles with assimilation. I have changed jobs frequently and didn't understand why. The reason seems to be that I continue to choose jobs that require almost complete assimilation. I have to make better choices.

I understand that my passion for law enforcement or aviation, one vocation in the past and one currently in place do not compare for my love of writing. It has only taken me 59 years to discover that.

Most importantly, I have had the responsibility for deciding my best friend's fate in getting him to stay the course in regards to our statement plan. How many people do you know that you would trust or would trust you with that kind of responsibility. I already knew that I had a brother. I already knew that I had a best friend. I know what I have and I appreciate it more now than ever. I got to join forces with the Mighty Musa and as Captain Jack would say, the story continues . . . .

EPILOGUE

Although this book is coming to a conclusion in this epilogue, I hope the reader has a better understanding of some of the challenging goals that lay ahead for all of America.

With these last few questions and comments, I am asking the reader to begin to take notice, because until we do individually and collectively, America will never be able to call itself great.

Jack: Joe, Where do think you best fit in both the Black and the White community?

Joe: While I can move quite comfortably in both groups, my personal comfort zone is somewhere between the two groups. A place I call the "gray area"; a place where you must have a high degree of self-worth to exist for any length of time, because there are not many who choose to reside there.

Jack: Joe, Why are you unable to find what you need within at least one of the groups?

Joe: Interesting enough, I have the same issues with both groups, they both lack the will for independent thinking. They seem to defer to others to do most of their critical thinking on important issues of our time, and set the agenda without their scrutiny. They are also left to argue about meaningless things like, who really won the super bowl, and who makes the best pickup truck.

It was now my turn to get asked some questions.

Joe: Jack, where do you think you best fit in the Black and White community?

Jack: I never looked at myself as having to "fit in" to either society. I think that most of my mind set about Black America, is the appalling thought that White America feels it has done "enough" toward equality.

Joe: Jack, what is one of your greatest challenges when it comes to Black America?

Jack: When I was very young, I thought "racist" jokes were funny. When I was older, I understood the "intent" of the "racist" jokes, but was not comfortable enough with myself to speak out against them. When I was "old enough", I came up with a very quick response to anything that resembled "racism". As soon as I knew a story was headed toward some "racist" comment, I would immediately stop the storyteller and say, "Did I tell you my best friend was Black?" Did I tell you that my good friend was Lebanese?, and so on. Not only were my comments absolutely true, it left most of the "storytellers" speechless. I then simply smiled and moved on to another subject. It still is a great way to diffuse this kind of thinking.

All that I am asking is for all of us to consider the possibility that additional information combined with our belief systems may create more positive outcomes. I know that Christopher Columbus certainly had more information to add to his beliefs, I know that Leonardo Da Vinci had more information to add to his beliefs, and I wish the state of Washington had taken the time to add to their beliefs . . . . knowledge and wisdom come from information and observing what is going on around us . . . . what a concept!

2012

Joe Washington still resides in the same community and is semi-retired. He still enjoys consulting. Joe Washington has remained my best friend and we talk on a regular basis. Joe has never looked back, does not belong to any "support" groups and carries on as a functional member of the community.